COLD

A History From Beginning to End

Copyright © 2016 by Hourly History

All rights reserved.

Table of Contents

Introduction

What Was the Cold War?

What was the Cold War? An easier question to answer might be, during the latter half of the twentieth century, what did the Cold War *not* encompass, especially for citizens of the United States and the Soviet Union? The Cold War was an ideological clash between two different economic systems, which were championed by two world superpowers. However, in reality, the Cold War forced people all over the world to grapple with differing ideas of freedom, human rights, the role of governments and democracy, wealth, the purpose and nature of culture, and more.

The Cold War is called the Cold War because it was technically "cold"l there was no direct fighting between the two major opponents. However, that did not mean that the war was bloodless or without victims. "Hot" fighting erupted in many corners of the globe - most famously, the United States involved itself in wars in Korea and Vietnam, and the Soviet Union was involved in fighting in China and Afghanistan.

However, blood was spilled elsewhere, too: revolutions (that often followed decolonization) in parts of Africa, Cuba, Latin America, Eastern Europe, and Asia caused millions of deaths. What is more, the United States and the Soviet Union often involved themselves in these affairs in pursuit of their own interests. More often than not, both sides became destabilizing forces and worsened situations in places like Guatemala and Eastern Europe.

Also, the Cold War had a serious impact on many people in the U.S. and the Soviet Union. The governments of both nations worked hard to convince citizens to define themselves against the other; for millions of people, these campaigns worked. The Cold War dictated the cultures of both countries. The governments of both used propaganda campaigns to demonize the other. People in America were afraid of Communists and hunted them, while the Soviets fiercely protected Communism and enforced their doctrines, painting America as a land of inequality and economic deprivation.

By so doing, the United States and the Soviet Union caused much suffering of their own people at home, especially for those who dared to publicly (and sometimes just privately) speak out against the actions of their own governments. The strict control of the government in the Soviet Union was legendary in the Western world. Many Soviet citizens lost their lives, and much more were displaced when they fled persecution. However, the United States was not immune either - they hunted Communists rabidly, rooting out those working in government and the public sector. As a consequence, many lost their jobs and careers and lost their reputations, families, and friends. Others lived in fear of repression. At times, violence broke out against dissidents.

The end of the Cold War was filled with historical moments that have come to epitomize its denouement in popular memory. These include the fall of the Berlin Wall, the breakup of the Eastern Bloc, and the end of Communism in Russia. The United States has been celebrated as the victor, but like most conflicts in global history, the end of the Cold War was more nuanced and complex. A variety of factors on both sides brought about its end. Also, while the Cold War enveloped so much of the U.S.'s and U.S.S.R.'s cultures and ways of life in the early decades of the conflict, as the years went on, in the 1970s and 1980s especially, this power and influence waned (at least in some realms of life).

The impact of the Cold War was far-reaching, and in some cases devastating. Its history is vital to understanding most events of the late twentieth century, virtually anywhere in the world.

Chapter One

The Origins of the Cold War

"This is a hooligan movement, young people run and shout that there is no bread, simply to create excitement, along with workers who prevent others from working. If the weather were very cold they would probably all stay home."

—Tsarina Alexandra

While the Cold War era did not begin until after World War II, its roots run much deeper throughout history. In Russia, centuries of oppression and class inequality made the promises of Communism appealing. It should be noted, however, that Russia's society did not possess many of the qualities that Karl Marx anticipated would lead to a Communist revolution, such as industrialization. In fact, feudalism—which is most commonly associated with the Middle Ages—had scarcely ended by the time the Russian Revolution broke out in the early twentieth century.

In the United States, perhaps the most important contributing factor to the Cold War was a deeply-held fear of radicalism that far pre-dated Communism. Americans had always been profoundly suspicious that a foreign, nefarious force was at work to undermine democracy and "freedom." Ironically, this fear often resulted in repression of some of America's most important and beloved rights, especially freedom of speech and freedom of the press. This kind of repression would continue to be a theme throughout the Cold War as well, despite rhetoric extolling those very virtues.

America's long-held fear of radicalism extended to Communism as early as the nineteenth century, shortly after Marx and Engels wrote many of their theoretical works. Throughout the late nineteenth century, as workers in America fought for their rights, the media (often owned by the very big businessmen that striking workers were fighting against) tarnished them as Communists. Even though many Americans did not necessarily understand what this meant, they learned to fear the name, just as they had feared change and other incarnations of radicalism in the past.

During World War I, America began a pattern of intervention against Communism, setting a dangerous precedent. When the Russian Revolution broke out, and it became clear that it was a Communist revolution, the United States attempted to undermine it. While America's role was not immediately apparent to all (and certainly it was not successful), it did create deep distrust between the two nations. This action would be repeated multiple times in the future: The United States would intervene during the Cold War again and again, around the world, to prevent the spread of Communism anywhere the U.S. government suspected it might be rising.

To make relations between Russia and the rest of the Western world worse, during World War I, because of the revolution, Russia signed a hasty treaty with Germany to get out of the war quickly. When Russia did this, it was not clear that Germany would lose the war. Russia's exit was worrisome, and even dangerous, for the rest of the countries fighting against Germany, especially France and Great Britain. This made the relationship between these nations tense as well.

During World War I, many countries – America included – worked to repress any class or labor unrest. The Russian Revolution occurred right in the middle of the war, heightening fears of Communism in other places. At the end of the war, as soldiers returned home and the affected areas reeled from the aftermath of the war, strikes broke out in several countries, creating a hysterical fear that a worldwide Communist conspiracy was at hand. Western nations especially feared that the revolution in Russia was spreading, causing a further rift between them and Russia.

In the United States, this fear manifested itself in the country's first Red Scare. The American government hunted Communists and suspected Communists. They deported many immigrants who were accused of Communist or radical sympathies without sound evidence. In one of this Red Scare's most infamous moments, the state of Massachusetts executed Italian radicals Nicola Sacco and Bartolomeo Vanzetti on weak evidence for murder; mostly, they were convicted because they were radicals (anarchists). All of this happened in the midst of massive culturally, politically, and socially conservative backlash in the country, which included a huge, nation-wide revival of the terrorist organization Ku

Klux Klan and the passage of Prohibition, which banned the sale and distribution of alcohol for more than a decade. This conservatism was only stemmed when the Great Depression necessitated a more liberal turn in government.

Americans familiar with their own history usually recognize the 1930s as the decade of the Great Depression, but in fact, the depression began earlier for most of the rest of the world. Many countries never fully recovered from World War I. Germany especially was crippled with war debt (one of the factors that contributed to Hitler's rise). After World War II, America would recognize that economic struggles made countries vulnerable to Communism. This was also true after World War I. Communism and leftist platforms became appealing to countries around the world. However, again, in America, conservatism reigned.

This would quickly change, however, when the depression visited America. During the 1930s, America softened on Communism in some ways. Although its numbers always remained well under one million people, membership in America's Communist Party reached its peak during the Depression. While still small numerically, the fact that more and more Americans were embracing Communism outright demonstrated that in general, leftist principles were more widely appealing and more accepted in the country.

What was more, in response to the suffering brought on by the Great Depression, the United States passed more liberal legislation, led by Democratic President

Franklin D. Roosevelt. Some of this legislation included the establishment of the Social Security Administration, which created an old-age pension for retired persons; massive public works projects, like the Tennessee Valley Authority, which brought electricity to much of rural America; and the Works Progress Administration, which employed thousands of artists, writers, and historians in promoting, preserving, and furthering aspects of American culture. All of this legislation met objections from the right; many accused Roosevelt and his fellow Democratic supporters of being socialists or Communists, but regardless of this kind of rhetoric, the legislation was popular, demonstrating America's "left turn."

Ironically (or perhaps not), Russia was escaping the effects of the Great Depression – one of the only places in the world that did. Because the Soviet Union was the only Communist country in the world at the time, it was not as connected to the global economy. After the Russian Revolution, the Russian government began massive plans to modernize, industrialize, and transition to Communism, which largely necessitated separation. At the same time, many countries hesitated to trade with or invest in the new Communist nation, some for economic and others for ideological reasons.

While this combination of factors helped insulate Russia from the effects of the worldwide depression, the industrializing mission of the early Communist government was also working. While certainly there was much violence and repression involved, Russia did undergo rapid industrialization in the wake of World War

I, which made it one of the only booming economies in the 1930s. Undoubtedly, this also made Communism more appealing in the United States and elsewhere around the world.

However, despite the example of Russia during the Great Depression, by the end of World War II, the United States and much of the Western world would again reject Communism and anything associated with it, this time with even greater furor than before. These fears would be a major contributing factor to the start of the Cold War.

Chapter Two

World War II and the Beginning of the Cold War

"The Red Army and Navy and the whole Soviet people must fight for every inch of Soviet soil, fight to the last drop of blood for our towns and villages...onward, to victory!"

—Joseph Stalin

While the causes of the Cold War are much more complex and long, the events leading up to, during, and the aftermath of World War II had much to do with the start of the Cold War.

First, there was deep distrust between the Soviets and the Americans during the war and the peace. Harry Truman was America's President at the end of the war, and for the first few years after, and he especially disliked and distrusted Stalin. Even though they were technically allies in the war, both were suspicious of the other. Historians almost universally agree that World War I and World War II are intricately connected, and really cannot be understood apart from one another. This meant that Russia's exit from World War I began a pattern of distrust that would carry over to World War II and beyond.

Another major factor contributing to the Soviet Union's alienation from the rest of the allies was that

Stalin and the Soviet Union had originally allied themselves with the Germans and Hitler during the inter-war period. It was only when Hitler decided to invade Russia that they became an Allied nation. Thus, the British and other Allied countries also distrusted the Soviets, even as they fought the war on the same side; the other Allies felt that the Soviets were forced to fight on their side, rather than choosing to side with them.

As previously stated, World War I and World War II were deeply connected events. The world thought that World War I was "the war to end all wars," but they were wrong: World War II caused far more death and destruction, involved more than one genocide, and impacted more nations and peoples than ever thought imaginable. Most recognized that World War I had been a contributing factor to the outbreak of World War II, therefore they also understood that the peace had to be very different. Thus, the way that World War II ended was transformative for the entire world. However, one thing was clear: the United States and the Soviet Union were the new superpowers.

Because of their deep distrust, and because of their ideological differences, these two superpowers became rivals wrapped in a dichotomy that would impact the entire world. Both saw each other and the rest of the world in black and white, so to speak. Both defined themselves against the other: whatever the Soviet Union was, or believed, or stood for, the United States was not, and vice versa.

Also, both saw the rest of the world in similar terms: either you were "with us or against us," meaning that other nations were either allied with capitalism *and* the United States, or Communism *and* the Soviet Union; there could be no other viable alternative. This was precisely why the Cold War had such far-reaching effects: The United States and the Soviet Union did not (and perhaps could not) fight each other directly. Instead, they fought for control and for allies everywhere else.

To make matters worse, this happened in the midst of rapid social and political change around the world. In the wake of World War II, major world powers gave up their global colonies in a process known as decolonization. Sometimes this happened voluntarily, when former colonizers gave up their colonies, but more often was the result of revolutionary movements in the colonies themselves. Since more and more countries and territories were gaining independence and forming new governments and economic systems, the United States and the Soviet Union had ample battleground.

The United States genuinely believed that Communism was like a virus: once one country was "infected" with Communism, it would spread and spread, to other countries. This became known as the Domino Theory: the belief that – like dominoes – one country's fall to Communism would cause another, and another, and another, until eventually the entire world would be infected with Communism, including the United States and her allies.

In the wake of World War II, the Domino Theory thus led to the American policy of Containment. To stop the spread of Communism (and its eventual spread to the United States), it needed to be contained where it was; it could not, under any circumstances, be allowed to spread beyond where it already existed. The Domino Theory and the policy of Containment became guiding foreign policy principles for the United States throughout the Cold War. They led the United States to intervene in other nations' affairs time and again.

In the immediate aftermath of World War II, the United States and the Soviet Union divided much of Europe, and some of the rest of the world, into spheres of influence. Since Russia had sacrificed so much more than the U.S. to end the war (far more civilian and combatant casualties and unspeakable damage to their infrastructure and land), there was no way that the U.S. could limit their role in the post-war world. Therefore, the U.S.S.R. oversaw the restructuring of most of Eastern Europe, as well as East Germany (and the eastern side of the capital city of Berlin).

Communist governments were created in much of Eastern Europe. The Soviet-aligned countries came to be known as the Eastern Bloc and included the U.S.S.R., Bulgaria, Czechoslovakia, East Germany, Hungary, Poland, Romania, and Yugoslavia (until the 1960s). The United States would attempt to spy on and undermine the governments of these countries throughout the Cold War. On the other hand, though, much of Western Europe was directly aligned with the U.S.: Belgium, Britain, Denmark,

Greece, Iceland, Italy, Luxembourg, the Netherlands, Norway, Turkey, and West Germany. Also, while Austria, France, Ireland, and Sweden were technically neutral, they were certainly more aligned with the Western Bloc. Only Switzerland and Finland managed to remain neutral; Europe was truly divided.

The United States developed specific policies that aimed at fighting the spread of Communism. The Marshall Plan was a major one. As Europe especially reeled in the wake of World War II, the United States and its allies in Europe (chiefly Great Britain) greatly feared that weaker nations were susceptible to falling to Communism. The widespread destruction and death, as well as resulting starvation and poverty, might make the doctrines of Communism appealing to a great many people. Therefore, under the Marshall Plan, the United States offered aid to any country needing it, provided that they were not affiliated with Communism. The Marshall Plan was directly related to the Domino Theory and Containment: its purpose was to prevent Communism from spreading anywhere else, and it aimed to win America more and more allies.

As discussed above, deep distrust divided the U.S. and the U.S.S.R. However, another factor during World War II widened this chasm: the dropping of the atomic bombs on Japan. To the Soviet Union, this made the United States a terrifying foe. While the Russians had been spying on America's nuclear program (the United States executed two of the spies for espionage, Julius and Ethel Rosenberg), they were not able to produce nuclear weapons yet. To make matters worse, the United States did not discuss their plans to use the bombs with the Soviet Union during the war. This set the precedent for a dangerous (not to mention exorbitantly expensive) arms race that continued through most of the Cold War.

Domestically, both nations began "fighting" the Cold War with their own citizens. Both countries developed means to not only spy on each other and compete but also to repress any discontent or non-conformity within their own countries. The actions of the Soviet investigative branch, the KGB, are legendary: many citizens were interrogated, imprisoned, or sent to labor camps for non-conformity with Communist doctrine.

In the United States, this ushered in a new Red Scare, arguably more severe and devastating than the first. Congress established the House Un-American Activities Committee (HUAC), whose purpose (in the beginning) was to root out Communists and Communist sympathizers working in any capacity for the federal government. Its most outspoken proponent was Senator Joseph McCarthy from Wisconsin (who took office in 1947), which is why the hunt for Communists during this era is often referred to as "McCarthyism."

Hundreds of employees were dragged in front of HUAC for questioning. Especially as the Red Scare went on and as the Committee became more powerful, the line of questioning was often unfair and certainly in violation of due process. Many people who were most likely innocent of any wrong-doing lost their jobs. What was more, these hearings were very public, so they also lost their reputations; their friends feared to associate with them, and some even lost the loyalty of their families. It is not an exaggeration to say that HUAC ruined many lives.

HUAC did not contain itself to federal employees or the public sector. It did not take long for them to begin investigating people working in other industries, including people working in Hollywood and other media outlets, including journalists. Infamously, a "Hollywood blacklist" emerged. No one could or would work with the actors, writers, directors, or other artists on it.

It also did not take long for HUAC's mission to spread as well. State and local governments began forming their own versions of this kind of committee to hunt Communists in their midst. Private companies as well took similar action, often instituting loyalty oaths and other means of enforcing conformity and loyalty. A new atmosphere of fear emerged that would haunt America for more than a decade. On the one hand, Americans feared anyone who was different or refused to conform in any way because they might be a threat to national security. However, on the other hand, people lived with a deep fear of being accused of being a Communist (which betrayed a knowledge that many accused were actually innocent). This shaped the way people acted and the decisions that they made, which had a huge impact on American life. This culture of conformity is more fully explored in chapter four.

In many ways, the 1940s shaped how the Cold War would progress, and the decade ended with a major blow to the United States. While Communism had existed in parts of China and had been an issue in their ongoing civil war, the country did not become Communist until 1949. China was massive in size, both regarding land and population. It was also strategically located. The Soviet Union now (ostensibly) had a major ally in Asia. Containment had failed, and America feared China's influence in the Eastern world. It would not be long before the United States would be embroiled in military conflict in Asia.

Chapter Three

The Cold War in the 1950s

"The only justification for repressive institutions is material and cultural deficit. But such institutions, at certain stages of history, perpetuate and produce such a deficit, and even threaten human survival."

—Noam Chomsky

The post-World War II environment of fear and distrust, as well as the policy of Containment, set the stage for the 1950s. In many ways, Americans are nostalgic about the 1950s; they picture hard-working fathers, loving yet submissive homemakers, carefree children, and prosperity. However, in reality, most Americans lived with extreme anxiety during the decade.

The culture of the Cold War will be more fully explored in the next chapter. However, it also worth touching on here as well. The Soviet Union had (and has) a terrible reputation for repression during the Cold War. However, the United States also had a culture of conformity and repression. It would not be until the 1960s that a viable challenge to this culture would emerge (though it was certainly attempted before). As discussed in the last chapter, fear of Communism led to a fear of being different and a fear of being accused of being a

Communist. This meant that individuals policed themselves and their families, often stifling individuality or cultural achievements.

America took Containment very seriously in the 1950s. China's fall to Communism was perceived as a major threat to American security. Thus, the country frequently intervened in other nations' affairs. Usually, this was through covert operations, as in Iraq in 1953 (see below). However, at times the Cold War turned hot, and U.S. troops went to war. One of the first instances was during the 1950s, in Korea. North Korea established itself as a Communist government, while South Korea remained capitalist, an ally of the West.

Then, in 1950, North Korea invaded South Korea, intending to reunite the country under one Communist government. North Korea had the support of the Chinese and (less outwardly) the Soviet Union. The United States led the United Nations' response to come to South Korea's aid. In the end, the war ended in a stalemate, and the status quo was maintained: North Korea and South Korea remained divided along the 38th parallel, and a demilitarized zone was created between the two. No treaty was signed, and the two are technically still at war.

However, like so many events in the Cold War, the Korean War was important for other reasons than just its immediate outcome. It set a precedent and showed both sides what the other was willing to do in such a situation. Importantly, no nuclear weapons were used, showing that warfare would not always resort to such destruction in the post-World War II era.

As stated above, intervention in other nations' affairs was common in the 1950s, and usually, this took the form of covert operations. "Covert operations" is a rather broad term, and can encompass everything from spying to outright paramilitary action. The U.S. and the Soviet Union both engaged in everything along this spectrum during the Cold War.

The goal of covert operations was often regime change. This meant overthrowing the current government and replacing it with one that leaders at the time think will be more friendly to their interests. One such incident has now become famous—the overthrow of Mohammed Mossadegh in Iran in 1953. Democratically elected, Mossadegh moved to nationalize the oil fields in that country. This action was perceived as an indicator of Communism by the West since nationalizing industry was something typical under Communist governments. Also, American and British businesses had a great deal of money invested in the oil industry in Iran. So, the United States' Central Intelligence Agency (along with British and other allies) overthrew Mossadegh (who was executed) and replaced him by reinstating the Shah. The Shah ran a corrupt and brutal government, which eventually led the Iranian people to revolution in the 1970s. While Americans remained oblivious to their government's actions in Iran for decades, the Iranian people were well aware, contributing to their dislike toward the United States and the Western world.

It was also during the 1950s that America first involved itself in Vietnam. Vietnam had been a French colony, and after the end of World War II fought for independence. The politics of the U.S. involvement in Vietnam is complicated, but suffice it to say that the U.S. government supported the regime of Ngo Din Diem initially. As in Iran, many Vietnamese people were unhappy with Diem, and revolutionary sentiment continued to fester.

These were the realms in which the U.S. and the Soviet Union fought during the Cold War – indirectly, for allies and sympathetic governments. While the U.S. and the Soviet Union obviously did not come to blows during the decade, there were tense moments. One of the most poignant was the Berlin Blockade and subsequent Berlin Airlift. The city of Berlin was located in East Germany, in the Soviet Bloc. However, because of the city's importance, it was divided into East and West Berlin, and even though it was located in the Soviet bloc, West Berlin was in the U.S.'s sphere of influence.

In a move meant to intimidate, the Soviet Union blockaded the city, meaning that West Berlin could not be accessed or supplied. In response, the U.S. and other Western countries flew planes over the city and dropped supplies of food and other necessities (as well as propaganda materials) via the air. In an embarrassing moment later on, Soviet Premier Khrushchev ordered the infamous Berlin Wall built between East and West Berlin.

Like in Korea, the Berlin Airlift had broader importance. The United States did not respond to Soviet provocation with military retaliation. All-out war did not occur. The Berlin Blockade and Airlift set another important precedent: the countries would fight, but not directly, even when tensions became very hot.

Another tense, crucial Cold War event was the continued growth of the arms race. In an occurrence that literally struck terror into the lives of most Americans, the Soviet Union successfully detonated an atomic bomb (thanks in part to spies within the American nuclear program). While the wake of World War II made everyone in the world weary of war and wary of more, the fact that both superpowers now had these weapons meant that direct military conflict surely would lead to mutual destruction.

A phenomenon and political philosophy known as Mutually Assured Destruction thus developed. It was exactly as its name implies: should the two main superpowers in the Cold War fight directly, both were assured complete destruction. This meant that the two powers could not come to blows directly. In an ironic twist, then, many at the time believed that arming themselves to the teeth would actually prevent rather than provoke warfare. Whether this was true or not, the two powers did not fight directly, though they did come close on more than one occasion.

In addition to the Soviet Union detonating an atomic weapon, an even more terrifying weapon was detonated by both sides during the 1950s—the hydrogen bomb. Much more powerful than the atomic weapons dropped on Japan to end World War II, the hydrogen bomb had the capability to destroy entire regions. This kind of weaponry made it even more apparent that the U.S. and the Soviet Union could not fight directly. The extent of death and destruction would be unthinkable.

The "Space Race" also began in the 1950s. Like the arms race, the United States and the Soviet Union competed over progress in this realm. Although the U.S. had a space program active at the time, the Soviets were successful in launching the first satellite into space, called Sputnik, in 1957. The ultimate goal of the Space Race was the moon landing, which the U.S. achieved first in 1969. Before then, competitions over sending humans into space and orbiting the earth also attracted much media attention as well as exorbitant amounts of public money for both the United States and the Soviet Union.

The Space Race infiltrated everyday life. American schools began emphasizing science and math in an effort to push young minds into those fields, and the Soviet government established special schools for the gifted. The preoccupation with space was also played out in popular culture. Television shows and movies featured space as a recurring theme. The science fiction genre took off in popularity. Moreover, Americans also developed a preoccupation with the idea of aliens, or life on other planets. Conspiracy theories about crashed intergalactic vessels were not uncommon.

In terms of foreign policy, and, in the 1950s, domestic policy, the United States was generally very conservative, in stark opposition to Soviet policies. At the same time, though, the 1950s were surprisingly liberal in other ways. President Dwight D. Eisenhower, the World War II general who directed the D-Day invasion, was only

Republican in name. He expanded many of Roosevelt's New Deal projects and created several new projects, like the building of the interstate highway system. So, the great irony of the decade was that while the United States took a very culturally conservative turn, the government charged with protecting this conservatism was actually becoming more liberal in some ways.

The 1950s also saw the fall of Joseph McCarthy, the spokesman of the government's manifestation of the Red Scare of the post-World War II era. McCarthy became a demagogue, alienating members of his own political party. He attacked the U.S. Army for allegedly harboring Communists. In response, the Senate investigated McCarthy and his accusations and ended up uncovering personal reasons that McCarthy attacked the army. He was censured, but his reputation was destroyed. He was dead within three years from alcoholism.

Certainly, there were some in government who did still fear liberalism and Communism, and the McCarthyism of the late 1940s outlived McCarthy himself. Liberals, dissidents, and intellectuals were hunted at the local and national levels in the United States and other NATO countries. Paranoia continued; local governments and even private businesses instituted loyalty oaths and other measures. Neighbors spied on each other and reported former friends to local investigative boards. Individuals and companies or groups were "black-listed," and anyone who spoke out against the blacklist was added to it. Most infamously, the Hollywood blacklist cost audiences the presence of many talented actors, writers, directors, and others involved in film-making. The House Un-American Activities Committee continued to hold hearings until 1975, investigating more people and costing more their jobs.

The people investigated by HUAC were obviously deeply impacted by the Cold War. However, even though they were the extreme, they were not alone. The Cold War's impact was felt by just about everyone since its cultural influence was vastly enormous. The culture of the Cold War will be more fully explored in the next chapter.

Chapter Four

The Culture of the Cold War

"The reason we have such a high standard of living is because advertising has created an American frame of mind that makes people want more things, better things, and newer things."

—Nikita Khrushchev

In large part, because victory in the Cold War was so hard to define, it permeated every aspect of life in the United States and the Soviet Union especially. This included elements of culture: movies, television, music, literature, how people dressed and lived their lives, and much more.

Many Americans remember the Cold War as a battle between freedom and oppression on many levels, including culture. Ostensibly, Americans enjoyed freedoms of expression that were not open to Soviet citizens because the government kept tight control over what was produced and what people were exposed to. They were not completely wrong about that: The Soviet Union did strictly control the cultural creations in its country, and other Eastern Bloc and Communist countries (like China) did as well. In the Soviet Union and other Eastern Bloc countries, the government largely owned the media outlets and often pre-screened the products that they did not produce.

However, cultural expression was not as free and open as most Americans would like to have believed. While the American government did not own movie studios or dictate what could and could not be said directly, they did have their own means of controlling the cultural atmosphere. We have already read about the House Un-American Activities Committee, but America policed itself in subtle ways also. Americans adopted what historians call a "culture of conformity." In essence, being different was dangerous, and men, women, and children all had strict expectations about how they should look and behave and live.

America saw itself as nothing if not the opposite of the Soviets. As Communism was on the far left of the political spectrum, America took a conservative turn in the wake of World War II that would last until the 1960s. Domestically, the "traditional" family became the ideal. Men were expected to work full-time jobs and provide for their families. Women were responsible for caring for their homes and raising happy, healthy, "normal" children. Finally, children were expected to represent their parents' work honorably: be obedient, and grow up to fulfill their appropriate roles as men and women, husbands and wives.

As you have read, the end of World War II brought a renewed boom in the economy. War production turned into consumer production, and as white Americans returned to work, they were expected to buy. Since

Communism was supposed to disregard materialism and consumer culture, America began to emphasize it. Happiness, in America, was expressed by what you owned. Consumerism was directly tied to the ideal of the "perfect" family described above: A successful husband provided his wife and children with a home in the suburbs, the newest appliances, two cars, mass-produced foods, and all of the things not available to Soviet families. Thus, that perfect family expressed itself as much by what it owned as how its members behaved.

We have already discussed in the previous chapter that being different—not fulfilling these prescribed gender, family, and social roles—was dangerous. If you were different, you might be a Communist. Thus, the phenomenon known as "Domestic Containment" emerged in the years after World War II. Just like the American government had a responsibility to contain Communism elsewhere in the world, all private citizens had a responsibility to contain Communism in their own lives, at home and in their communities. As previously presented, this led Americans to accuse each other of Communism and created a "witch hunt" atmosphere. However, it also permeated home life and placed tremendous pressure on women especially.

Women, whose chief role was wife and mother, were solely responsible for the physical, social, and moral health of their families. Put simply, this meant that if there was something "wrong" with any member of the family (if they failed to uphold the standards set for them by Cold War society), then it was the fault of the matriarch. This was one of the major problems with the culture of conformity, and would lead to the Feminist Movement in the 1960s and 1970s.

Not only women were negatively impacted by the culture of conformity. It is important to pause here and take note that these standards only applied to a certain subset of American people. Notably, African-Americans were left out of this image, completely absent from advertising and often excluded from programs that made these things available. White families left the cities to live in the suburbs in a phenomenon known as white flight, and the neighborhoods they fled to intentionally excluded African Americans.

During World War II, African-Americans served in the United States military in astonishing numbers, representing a much higher proportion than whites in relation to their presence in the general population, even though they were forced to serve in segregated units. Returning black GIs and their families expected that, finally, they had earned equality through this service. However, the majority of white Americans, especially Southern whites, opposed any extension of civil rights to black Americans and worked to maintain the status quo.

The Civil Rights Movement was born in the aftermath of World War II. It was a long, momentous struggle, and is the subject of other books. However, it was important in the Cold War because of its international implications. America painted itself as the arbiter of freedom; the image that the U.S. tried to create for itself was that of the protector of liberty against Communism's and the

U.S.S.R.'s repressive tendencies. However, as news and footage of the Civil Rights Movement was transmitted around the world, America appeared hypocritical. How could it purport to protect these rights and freedoms abroad if it did not ensure them for all its own citizens? What was more, many of the countries that the U.S. was trying to influence were located in South America, Asia, and Africa. Rampant, violent racism did not exactly endear Americans to people of color elsewhere in the world, many of whom had also suffered the effects of racism on the part of white Westerners.

Black Americans were obviously (and rightfully) critical of the culture of conformity. However, they were not alone. Even before the "hippie" movement (or the rise of the New Left) in the late 1960s, some groups and movements did attempt to undermine the culture of conformity as well. One of these groups was known as the "Beatniks," or the "Beats." This group of young artists and writers and poets wandered, and were disillusioned with the culture of conformity and domestic containment. Some of the famous Beats were the poet Alan Ginsberg and the author Jack Kerouac, whose book *On the Road* epitomized the lifestyle and mindset of the Beats.

Also, liberal intellectuals saw a danger in mass consumption and conformity, and they recognized that McCarthyism violated basic American rights. Artists and thinkers especially worried that creativity and individuality would be lost, ruining American culture. How could great works of literature, innovative music, or advances in thought and philosophy be produced if no one knew how to think for themselves?

The years following World War II were thus culturally conservative in the United States. At times, the culture of conformity was repressive, silencing opposition, and stifling creativity and individualism. In many ways, it violated ideals Americans held dear: freedom of speech and expression. It also undermined the image America created of itself abroad, that American freedoms allowed creativity and innovation to flourish.

Despite worries and attempts to undermine it, and despite the fact that it was antithetical in many ways to America's own ideals, this cultural atmosphere would perpetuate well into the 1960s. In many ways, it would take a myriad combination of factors to reveal its problems and begin to destroy it: discontent among many groups of Americans, the growing violence against the Civil Rights movement, protest against the war in Vietnam, and economic depression. All of these factors are discussed in the ensuing chapters.

Chapter Five

The Cold War in the 1960s

"Don't you understand, what I'm trying to say? And can't you feel the fear that I'm feeling today? If the button is pushed there's no running away. There'll be no one to save with the world in a grave. Take a look around you, boy, it's bound to scare you, boy. But you tell me over and over and over and over again my friend. Ah, you don't believe we're on the eve of destruction."

—Barry McGuire, Eve of Destruction

Many people think of 1960s America as the decade of the "hippies": anti-war protests, free love, new music, et cetera. However, in reality, this culture did not emerge until very late in the decade. Most of the 1960s closely resembled what many people popularly remember as the 1950s. However, the momentous decade would shake America's Cold War foundation, revealing many of its problems and hypocrisies. In many ways, the 1960s represented a turning point in the Cold War for the United States, the Soviet Union, and the rest of the world.

Before the war in Vietnam captured America's attention (and ire), events in Cuba were much more prominent, for both the U.S. and Russia. In January 1959, Fidel Castro and the July 26 Movement seized power, ousting the U.S.-supported Batista government. Initially, the revolution and the new government were not necessarily Communist, however.

America's treatment of Cuba in the wake of its revolution is emblematic of its foreign policy problems during the Cold War. Cuba and Castro were no fans of the Soviet Union initially; in fact, Castro did not want to ally his new government with them. He wanted greater independence, rather than living under the shadow of one of the world's superpowers again (the United States had loomed over Cuba since independence at the end of the nineteenth century, largely controlling and exploiting its economy and influencing its culture). However, when Cuba adopted left-leaning policies and practices, the U.S. cut off sugar imports from Cuba, crippling Cuba's economy. Fearing an economic meltdown, Castro was forced to turn to the Soviet Union to not only buy their sugar but also to provide crucial imports that had previously come from the United States. He also believed that he needed to defend his small island nation against possible attacks from a hostile U.S., and fatefully began purchasing arms from the Soviets.

It is very dangerous to speculate about "what-if" scenarios in history. However, it is relatively safe to say that, had America been able to see past the dichotomy of "us versus them," and understand that there was a third option for developing nations besides siding with the U.S. and the Soviet Union (siding with neither completely, but rather occupying some in-between or outside ideological space), they may have prevented the drama that ensued between the two neighbor nations.

However, this was not the course taken by the United States. Instead, the U.S. aimed to overthrow Fidel Castro's government and assumedly introduce a new leader friendly to America and capitalism, even if he be unpopular with the Cuban people. The CIA made several attempts on Castro's life, ranging from the serious to the almost comical (sending him poison cigars). Fidel Castro was a very smart revolutionary leader, and he knew not to take the U.S. threat lightly. In some ways, he was thus thrust into the lap of the Soviet Union. He knew that his country and he himself needed protection from a larger nation, and since the U.S. and U.S.S.R. were so diametrically opposed to one another, the Soviets came knocking.

Given that Castro's government adopted some left-leaning policies, such as land seizure and redistribution (some from American-owned companies), America thought that it was only a given that Cuba had "chosen sides" with the Soviet Union. Thus, America began actively spying on Cuba, as well as developing programs to undermine Castro's government. Before leaving office, President Eisenhower officially cut off ties with Cuba.

While President John F. Kennedy, who assumed the presidency in 1961, was a Democrat, like his Republican predecessor he was a "Cold Warrior," meaning he was tough on Communism. He believed that they needed to be subdued in order to keep the United States safe. So, continuing the work of Kennedy's predecessor, the CIA trained a paramilitary force partially made up of Cuban exiles to invade the island. In April 1961, they did just that, in the infamous Bay of Pigs invasion.

The invasion was a consummate disaster. Within only three days, the 1,400 U.S.-trained and funded troops surrendered. They were publicly captured, interrogated, and imprisoned. The U.S. involvement was obvious, and it was an embarrassment on the global stage. What was more, U.S. goals were not only not met, but undermined. The invasion made Castro more popular than ever in Cuba and strengthened his regime and the Cuban people's support for it. What was more, the Bay of Pigs set the stage for the Cuban Missile Crisis.

The Cuban Missile Crisis, as it came to be known, was the closest that the Soviet Union and the United States came to actual, all-out war. It was terrifying for those who lived through it. After the Bay of Pigs fiasco, the U.S. continued to work on ways to overthrow Castro. Through spying, the Soviet Union found out and alerted Cuba. In response, the Soviets and Cubans began plans to erect missile silos on the island.

It was not long before the United States discovered these structures, again by spying on their island neighbor. They were terrified. Nuclear weapons so close to home was not something that U.S. citizens had experienced in the past, and Kennedy took a hard line. He demanded that Soviet vessels carrying the weapons turn around, and if they did not, he implied that nuclear war might ensue. In a tense few days of negotiations, Kennedy finally agreed to remove U.S. nuclear weapons in Turkey, and the Soviets turned back.

In response to the very real danger the world faced during these thirteen days in 1962, disarmament took center stage. Both the U.S. and the Soviet Union scaled back on their arms races. In the U.S. especially, domestic issues demanded more focus from government leadership, as the Civil Rights Movement reached new proportions and President Lyndon Johnson, Kennedy's successor (after Kennedy was assassinated in 1963), made Civil Rights a priority of his administration.

Partially in response to the Cuban Missile Crisis, the Kremlin moved to replace Khrushchev, and in 1964, he was forced to step down. More moderate leadership took his place, and détente became a guiding foreign policy philosophy. Détente was an all-encompassing term that essentially meant that Cold War tensions and conflict would be scaled back. Nations around the world embraced non-alignment, by joining the Non-Aligned Movement or OPEC rather that openly associate with either the Soviets or the Americans. France left NATO.

However, certainly, the Cold War did not cease to be a guiding issue for both nations. Early in his presidency, before the Cuban Missile Crisis, Kennedy founded the Peace Corps. This organization sent young Americans to developing countries to help on projects like cultivating food, building schools and education, et cetera. Ostensibly, they did this as representatives of U.S. altruism, but in reality, it was very much tied to the Cold War. The battle for hearts and minds was very real, and

Kennedy and his advisors believed that the Peace Corps would spread good will toward America and win allies in developing countries.

It was also during the1960s that one of the most poignant events of the Cold War began: America's Vietnam War. While U.S. involvement in Vietnam dated back farther than Kennedy's presidency, it was during the 1960s that the United States really got involved. During Kennedy's presidency, the United States orchestrated the coup of Diem's government, and he was subsequently assassinated. Afterward, as North Vietnam attempted to unite South Vietnam under Communism, the United States escalated its military involvement. At first, troop commitment was low, but as the decade wore on, more and more American soldiers were sent to Vietnam.

In retrospect, it is now easy to see that from the beginning, the U.S. goals were not being met. At the time, the United States used military tactics that had worked traditionally in other places. However, the North Vietnamese used guerrilla tactics which United States forces were unprepared for. What was more, they did not adapt their tactics.

The events of the Vietnam War were complex and have filled many books. One of the most important elements of the war to understand now, though, is that of escalation. As the war wore on, the United States became more and more determined not to lose. Congress gave President Johnson hugely flexible war powers, and more and more troops were committed to the war, which military leaders always believed was possible.

The war was not unpopular in the beginning. Americans were accustomed to recognizing that Communism was a serious threat, and preventing it from spreading in Vietnam very much fit into this mission. However, as death tolls rose, more and more Americans began to question their involvement in the war. What was more, the Vietnam War was America's first major engagement that took place after most homes had televisions. This meant that millions were watching the destruction like never before every day. Attitudes began to turn.

Late in the decade, anti-war sentiment erupted. Young Americans especially protested America's involvement in the war. At the same time, Americans became horrified by the worsening violence against the Civil Rights Movement. Also, Americans were also growing more and more discontented with the culture of conformity. Young people rejected the expectations that their parents and society placed on them. Although the "hippies" were not numerous, many young Americans accepted that major changes needed to occur.

Vietnam became such a disaster for President Johnson that he decided not to run for re-election in the 1968 presidential race. During the election, some of the protest movements erupted in violence, especially in the wake of the assassinations of several prominent leaders, including civil rights leader Dr. Martin Luther King, Jr. Americans ended up electing conservative leader Richard Nixon. Between 1968 and the middle of the 1970s, America would change dramatically, and the direction of the Cold War would as well.

Chapter Six

The Cold War in the 1970s

"The greatest honor history can bestow is that of peacemaker."

—Richard Nixon

During the 1970s, the détente of the late 1960s continued between the United States and the Soviet Union. After Khrushchev was ousted from power, Leonid Brezhnev took over. He was more moderate than his predecessor, often relying on his advisers before making any foreign or domestic policy decisions.

One of the most iconic moments of the Cold War 1970s was Nixon's historic visit to China. China fell to Communism in 1949, and since then, relations between the United States and the West were strained, with limited communications and trade. Nixon's visit changed this. On the most basic level, it re-opened relations between the two major powers. However, it was far more significant. It showed that the U.S. could finally open talks and relations with a Communist nation apart from the Soviet Union. For the first time, America acknowledged that Communism did not automatically mean that a nation was allied with the Soviets. This was a major turning point in the Cold War.

Partially because of Nixon's visit to China, the Soviet Union also moved to soften relations with the United States. In another historic Cold War moment, Nixon and Brezhnev met. They signed the first in a series of agreements to limit the arms race. The Strategic Arms Limitation Treaty, or SALT I, limited the kinds of and numbers of weapons both countries could possess and develop.

Neither nation took SALT I entirely seriously; in ensuing years, it would become obvious that both violated their promises. However, like Nixon's visit to China, it was significant in other ways. Just the acknowledgment, on both sides, that weapons should be limited was an important milestone in itself. What was more, the two leaders of the two superpowers were actually sitting down and talking. In some ways, the Iron Curtain came up just a little bit.

At the same time, though, Nixon was still a "Cold Warrior," and many of the decisions he made during his presidency aimed to weaken the Soviet Union and promote the political, cultural, and economic interests of the Cold War.

Most importantly, he escalated the war in Vietnam. He began secret bombing of Cambodia, which eventually caused a civil war in that country that killed at least one million people. As the early years of the decade wore on, it became clear that the war in Vietnam was unwinnable. American support for the war was virtually non-existent. America pulled almost all of its troops by mid-decade, and in 1975, Saigon, the seat of South Vietnam's government, fell to North Vietnam.

In part, Vietnam exemplified the problems of both the United States and the Soviet Union in the Cold War. Both countries interfered in the affairs of other parts of the world, unsettling countries and destabilizing governments, causing destruction and death and revolution and civil war, just in the name of allies. It was a dangerous game; in many ways, the Cold War *was* a war of attrition: attrition of allies. While Vietnam should have taught important lessons, the United States continued to interfere in the affairs of other countries, as did the Soviet Union. In less than five years, the Soviet Union would itself be embroiled in its own Vietnam: Afghanistan.

It was not only in Vietnam that the Cold War also escalated in other parts of the world. Despite improved relations in some ways, the U.S. and the Soviet Union competed for allies and involved themselves in conflicts in the Middle East and South and Central America. Also, the U.S. publicized atrocities committed against Soviet citizens, especially well-known public figures such as writer Aleksandr Solzhenitsyn. By the late 1970s, relations between the two superpowers had again deteriorated. Despite another SALT treaty signed by President Jimmy Carter in 1979, tensions between the two more closely resembled the 1950s by the beginning of the next decade.

Besides détente, the Cold War shifted during the 1970s in other ways. Economically, a phenomenon known as "stagnation" hit the United States as well as the Soviet Union. Previously, the economies of both countries, especially the U.S., had been strong. However, worldwide, the economies of both countries stalled. Many Americans and other Westerners lost their jobs. In the Soviet Union, many people worked for very little and could not feed their families. The population of both superpowers grew more and more discontented; perhaps they were not as powerful as they had been taught.

The stagnant economy contributed to a sense of malaise during the decade. Americans especially became disenchanted with the unfulfilled promises of the culture of conformity and prosperity. The world was ready for change, and the 1980s would bring it.

Chapter Seven

The Cold War in the 1980s and the End of the Cold War

"You and I have a rendezvous with destiny. We will preserve for our children this, the last best hope of man on earth, or we will sentence them to take the first step into a thousand years of darkness."

—Ronald Reagan, 1964

The world entered the 1980s with a sense of disenchantment. Many places in the world were (very publicly) at war, or suffering the effects of violence and governmental instability. Leaders in both the United States and the Soviet Union – most notably, Ronald Reagan and Mikhail Gorbachev – recognized this, and worked to reinvigorate their people. While the Cold War was certainly approaching its end during the 1980s, that did not mean that the Cold War "cooled off." On the contrary, relations between the U.S. and the Soviet Union actually worsened a great deal during the 1980s, continuing the trend began in the late 1970s.

During the 1970s, the U.S. had many domestic issues. On top of that, President Jimmy Carter made human rights a main foreign policy priority. For the first time since World War II, the U.S. focused its energies on a foreign policy issue besides Communism. However, in 1980 America elected Ronald Reagan, who was an old Cold Warrior – he was an actor who began his political career accusing fellow Hollywood-ers of harboring Communist sympathies. During his presidency, he once again made Communism and the Soviet Union especially his top priorities.

It was no secret when Ronald Reagan took office that the Soviet Union was struggling economically. Therefore, Reagan and his administration sought to do everything in their power to make matters worse. He and his advisers believed that by initiating a massive arms race, the U.S. could spend the Soviet Union into bankruptcy. Despite signing another SALT treaty with Gorbachev, the arms build-up (especially the nuclear arms build-up) accelerated at an alarming rate.

In reality, the Soviet economy and society were much more complex, and a mere arms race probably did not bring about the end of the Soviet Union, but certainly, it did not help. More important to the end of the Cold War was the Soviet war in Afghanistan. America saw the war in Afghanistan as the Soviet Union's Vietnam, and in many ways, it was: the Soviets were fighting a guerrilla war in a harsh natural environment (Afghanistan is very rocky and mountainous) with which they were unfamiliar, while the enemy was very familiar with the terrain. In many ways, the Soviets also greatly misunderstood the ideological background of the peoples who populated Afghanistan, much like the U.S. had in Vietnam.

America was not content to sit idly by and allow matters in Afghanistan to run their course. Rather, they began secretly smuggling valuable, destructive weapons to the group fighting the Soviets: the Mujahedeen. The irony is that the Mujahedeen would in the future provide the historical roots of the Taliban and Al Qaeda; one of their leaders was Osama bin Laden, the mastermind behind the September 11, 2001 terror attacks on the U.S.

Other crises peppered the 1980s before the end of the Cold War. Another major crisis occurred in the 1980s. While this was not well-known among civilians at the time, it was probably as dangerous as the Cuban Missile Crisis; at least the closest that the world had come to nuclear war since that event. It is known as the Able Archer Crisis and recently declassified documents have made us aware of it.

During the Able Archer Crisis, America began exercises in preparation for nuclear war. The Soviets intercepted and observed what was going on. Because communication between the two countries was not good at the time, the Soviet Union did not attempt to contact the United States to find out what was going on, nor had the U.S. made the Soviets aware. Therefore, the Soviet government believed that the U.S. was actually readying itself for nuclear war. In retaliation, they too began to prepare to launch their weapon stores. Actual nuclear war was narrowly avoided when the two superpowers finally communicated and realized what was happening.

The United States also returned to a pattern of intervention in other countries that had at least slowed in the late 1970s. Most notably, Reagan supported the Nicaraguan Contras, a guerrilla military force that sought to undermine the Communist government, despite their brutality. Even after Congress expressly forbade his administration from giving them any support, he continued to do so. In what came to be known as the Iran-Contra Affair, Reagan secretly sold weapons illegally to Iran (an action which had been banned) and used the money to fund the Contras. When the scandal broke in the mid-1980s, however, several of Reagan's advisers and members of his administration took the fall. Reagan's reputation recovered relatively unscathed, helping earn him the nickname "the Teflon President." However, the Nicaraguans especially were not as lucky; once again, U.S. intervention had caused turmoil, and further death and destruction.

By the time Reagan's vice president George Bush won the election in 1988 and took office in 1989, the Soviet Union was weak. Within the year, the government collapsed, the Eastern Bloc broke up, and the Berlin Wall came down. The Cold War was officially over. Entire generations of the people alive at the time had lived their entire lives with hatred and fear of the other side, and probably with the belief that the long conflict would never end. The coming years would shape the post-Cold War world, but its legacy is still felt now, in the new millennium.

Conclusion

The Legacy of the Cold War

The Cold War lasted for more than forty years. Generations of people were born and raised in its shadow. Even though the Cold War officially ended in 1989 when the Soviet Union broke up, its legacy lasted a very long time.

Many countries who were aligned with either the U.S. or the Soviet Union still maintain a Cold War mentality when it comes to foreign policy. They believe that other countries are either allies or enemies, and they try to make complicated relationships fit into those narrow parameters.

In many ways, the United States has not learned diplomatic lessons from the Cold War. During George W. Bush's presidency, in the wake of the September 11 terror attacks, the president issued what has come to be known as the Bush Doctrine. In it, he dedicated the country to finding and destroying terrorism wherever it existed. Importantly, he took a decidedly "you're either with us or with them" attitude – the same attitude that caused much misunderstanding and destruction during the Cold War. The former Soviet Union, Russia, has struggled politically in the aftermath of the Cold War. It has had difficulty establishing a stable government and upholding human rights. It has also struggled to establish a place for itself on the world stage.

The Cold War also left an indelible mark on culture. You have read how the Cold War dictated culture for at least a decade, and arguably much longer. The remnants of that time are with us. Ironically, many are nostalgic for this time, which in reality was fraught with problems.

In a way, it may even be arguable that Americans and other Westerners (especially the British) romanticize the Cold War. It seems like a simpler time when the "enemy" was clearly and easily identifiable. In some people's minds, this stands in stark contrast to the "enemies" of today, who are very often stateless and use non-traditional means of fighting, namely, terrorism.

What is more, culturally, we are presently seeing a revival of fascination with the Cold War. Several successful television series and films have focused on the era, emphasizing especially espionage on both sides. There has also been an abundance of films made about space exploration, indicating that again we are turning our attention to the stars, and in a reinvigorated space race.

More than twenty years after its end, historians are still grappling with the Cold War and the many, many events that occurred during these years. The Cold War shaped the nature of culture, politics, economics, and more for over forty years. Undoubtedly, we will continue to learn more about it as time marches on.

Made in the USA
Middletown, DE
07 December 2018